LIVING IN... AUSTRALIA

by Chloe Perkins
illustrated by Tom Woolley

READY-TO-READ

SIMON SPOTLIGHT

An imprint of Simon & Schuster Children's Publishing Division • New York London Toronto Sydney • 1230 Avenue of the Americas, New York, New York 10020 • This Simon Spotlight edition March 2017 • Text copyright © 2017 by Simon & Schuster, Inc. • Illustrations copyright © 2017 by Tom Woolley • All rights reserved, including the right of reproduction in whole or in part in any form. SIMON SPOTLIGHT, READY-TO-READ, and colophon are registered trademarks of Simon & Schuster, Inc. For information about special discounts for bulk purchases, please contact Simon & Schuster Special Sales at 1-866-506-1949 or business@simonandschuster.com.
Manufactured in the United States of America 0117 LAK 10 9 8 7 6 5 4 3 2 1
Library of Congress Cataloging-in-Publication Data
Names: Perkins, Chloe, author. | Woolley, Tom, 1981- illustrator. Title: Australia / by Chloe Perkins ; illustrated by Tom Woolley. Description: First Simon Spotlight hardcover/paperback edition. | New York : Simon Spotlight, 2017. Series: Living in . . . | Series: Ready-to-read | Audience: K to grade 3. Identifiers: LCCN 2016018598 | ISBN 9781481480932 (hardcover) | ISBN 9781481480925 (paperback) | ISBN 9781481480949 (eBook) Subjects: LCSH: Australia—Juvenile literature. Classification: LCC DU96.P46 2017 | DDC 994—dc23
LC record available at https://lccn.loc.gov/2016018598

GLOSSARY

Aborigines: native peoples of Australia who settled the Australian continent in prehistoric times

commonwealth: a country that mostly acts on its own, but is partly ruled by or connected to another country because the two countries have common interests and goals

continent: the largest bodies of land on Earth; there are seven continents

cricket: a popular game in Australia that is somewhat similar to baseball

independent: describes a person, place, or thing that is not controlled by or supported by someone or something else

inland: describes any place that is not close to an ocean or sea

land bridge: a strip of land that acts like a bridge, connecting two places

NAIDOC Week: a weeklong event held in Australia each July to celebrate the history, culture, and achievements of Aboriginal and Torres Strait Islander peoples; NAIDOC stands for National Aborigines and Islanders Day Observance Committee

outback: much of central, northern, and western Australia where few people live and the land is wild

rugby: a popular game in Australia that is similar to American football

settler: a person who leaves his or her home to live in a new place, usually to create a new colony, or community, for his or her people

Torres Strait Islanders: native people of Australia who settled the Torres Strait Islands in prehistoric times

Hello! My name is Ruby,
and I live in Australia.
Australia is a country where
more than twenty-two million
people live . . .
including me!

Australia is not just a country.
It's a continent, too!
The Earth has seven continents.
Continents are the largest
bodies of land on Earth.
More than eight thousand
islands are also part of
our country.

TORRES
STRAIT
ISLANDS

AUSTRALIA

TASMANIA

On the continent of Australia,
there are tropical rain forests in
the northeast. In the southeast and
southwest you will find many farms.
Along the east coast are mountains
called the Great Dividing Range.
Australia's tallest mountain
is part of this range!

Most of western and central
Australia is called the outback.
Very few people live in the outback,
and the land there is mostly wild.
At the center of the outback is
Uluru (say: OO-loo-roo), a
rock formation that is sacred
to the native people of Australia.

The outback is home to many interesting animals, such as the kangaroo, the koala, and the emu. Not all of the animals in the outback are cute and fluffy, though.

Some of the most dangerous snakes and spiders on Earth call Australia home too.

Most Australians live in cities along the coast, but Australia's capital city, Canberra, is farther inland. Perth is on the west coast of Australia. It has one of the biggest inner-city parks in the world! The park is even bigger than New York City's famous Central Park!

Sydney is famous for its opera house designed by Jørn Utzon (say: yorn OOT-sun). He got the idea for its design as he was peeling an orange! Melbourne is the center for sports. Many Australians love to play cricket, rugby, and soccer!

I live on the eastern coast of Australia in a town called Byron Bay.
I live in a house with my grandma and grandpa.
I have one older brother named Teddy.

My grandma is an artist.
She paints pretty pictures
and works at an art store
near the beach.
My grandpa is a plumber.
He makes sure people have water
for their homes. My brother is
away at college in Brisbane,
a city about two hours away.

My grandma wakes me up
each morning before school.
I put on a skirt and my
special school uniform shirt.
After I get dressed, I brush my
teeth and comb my hair.
Then I meet my grandparents
in the kitchen for breakfast.

Today we eat eggs and toast. Then my grandma brings out a special treat that we usually save for tea time—lamingtons!

Lamingtons are little sponge cakes covered in chocolate frosting and coconut. Yummy!

After breakfast my grandpa drives
me to school on his way to work. Our
school year lasts from late January
until mid-December. We have summer
vacation in December. Australia is in
the southern hemisphere, so our
seasons are the opposite of those in
North America, Europe, and much of
Asia, too.

There are eighteen students
in my class. We study English,
math, science, computers, gym,
social studies, and creative arts,
such as acting, drawing, and dancing.
Our first subject this morning
is social studies. We are learning
about the history of Australia.

Fifty thousand years ago
the ocean around Australia
was not as deep as it is today.
People likely came to Australia
by land bridges and boats.
Today these people are known as
the Australian Aborigines and
Torres Strait Islanders.

Aborigines came to the continent
of Australia before ocean levels
rose. The Torres Strait Islanders
traveled a similar path, but they
settled in the Torres Strait Islands.
The Aborigines were hunter-gatherers,
which means they hunted animals
and gathered wild plants for food.

Aborigines did not have writing,
so they passed knowledge
down to their children through
songs, dances, and spoken stories.
As time passed, the Aboriginal
population grew to 750,000 people.
More than seven hundred languages
were spoken throughout the land.

Starting in the year 1500, people from other parts of the world began sailing to Australia. In 1770, Captain James Cook arrived and claimed Australia for Great Britain. The first group of British settlers arrived in 1788, and more followed.

The settlers fought the Aborigines
for their land. The Aborigines fought
back, but many of them were sick
with diseases that the settlers had
brought with them. Over the next
two hundred years, settlers stole
the Aborigines' land and took
away most of their rights.

By 1829, Great Britain had taken over nearly all of Australia. News of jobs and cheap land brought in even more settlers. As time passed, towns such as Sydney and Melbourne grew into big cities. Railroads were built to help people travel more quickly.

Great Britain declared Australia an independent Commonwealth in 1901. This meant that Australia became a country with its own government and its own laws, but Great Britain still had the final say over many of the Commonwealth's decisions. Australia became fully independent in 1986.

In 1962, Aborigines and Torres Strait Islanders fought hard for and won the right to vote. The government began helping Aborigines buy back the land that had been stolen from them. Today, Aboriginal and Islander cultures are celebrated during NAIDOC Week every July.

After our social studies lesson,
we study math and English. Look!
I got a good score on my spelling test.
The way English words are spelled
in Australia is sometimes different
from how they are spelled in the US.
See? We spell the word "color"
with a *u*—"colour."

Now it's lunchtime! I am eating a ham
and cheese sandwich. My friend
is eating a sandwich filled with
Vegemite, a tasty salty spread.
My grandpa packs me a lunch, and
sometimes he gives me money so that
I can buy a treat at the canteen.
A canteen is a little shop in the
lunchroom where you can buy food.

After lunch I have science class,
computer class, and art class. Then
it's time to go home! My grandma
picks me up, and we walk to
the art store where she works.

Then we go to the back of the shop
to unwrap some new paintings.
These paintings were done by an
Aboriginal artist of the Arakwal
(say: ah-ROCK-wall) people.
The Arakwal people have lived
in Byron Bay for more than
22,000 years!

When my grandma is done working, we take a walk along the beach. My favorite thing about living in Australia is surfing. I have been surfing for two years now. Surfing is a popular sport in Australia because many beaches have a lot of big waves.

My favorite surfer is
Layne Beachley. She won
seven world championships
between 1998 and 2006!
Some of Beachley's world records for
surfing still have not been broken.

Grandpa picks us up from the beach, and I wash up before dinner. Tonight we are grilling steak on the barbecue. My grandma makes a salad, too. After dinner we have a video chat with my brother in Brisbane. It's so nice to visit with him!

After we say good-bye, I finish my
homework and get ready for bed.
I have posters on my walls of
beaches in Hawaii, Mexico, and
South Africa. I would like to
surf at all of them when I grow up.
Would you like to visit
Australia someday?

ALL ABOUT
AUSTRALIA!

NAME: Commonwealth of Australia (or Australia for short!)

POPULATION: 22.75 million   **CAPITAL:** Canberra

LANGUAGE: Most people in Australia speak English, but Mandarin, Italian, Arabic, Greek, Cantonese, and Vietnamese are also spoken. Aboriginal Australians and Torres Strait Islanders speak many other different languages!

TOTAL AREA: 2,988,901 square miles

GOVERNMENT: Federal parliamentary democracy and a Commonwealth realm

CURRENCY: Australian dollar

FUN FACT: Many famous actors grew up in Australia, including Nicole Kidman, Hugh Jackman, Cate Blanchett, Russell Crowe, and Chris and Liam Hemsworth.

FLAG: Dark blue with the flag of the United Kingdom in the upper left side, below which is a seven-pointed star. On the right side of the flag are more stars in the shape of the Southern Cross constellation that can be seen in Australia's night sky.